CREATING SURPLUS VALUE FOR CUSTOMERS.

CREATING SURPLUS VALUE FOR CUSTOMERS

By: D.K. Hawkins
Version 1.1 ~November 2022
Published by D.K. Hawkins at KDP
Copyright ©2022 by D.K. Hawkins. All rights reserved.

No part of this publication may be reproduced, distributed, or transmitted in any form or by any means including photocopying, recording, or other electronic or mechanical methods or by any information storage or retrieval system without the prior written permission of the publishers, except in the case of very brief quotations embodied in critical reviews and certain other noncommercial uses permitted by copyright law.

All rights reserved, including the right of reproduction in whole or in part in any form.

All information in this book has been carefully researched and checked for factual accuracy. However, the author and publisher make no warranty, express or implied, that the information contained herein is appropriate for every individual, situation, or purpose and assume no responsibility for errors or omissions.

The reader assumes the risk and full responsibility for all actions. The author will not be held responsible for any loss or damage, whether consequential, incidental, special or otherwise, that may result from the information presented in this book.

All images are free for use or purchased from stock photo sites or royalty-free for commercial use. I have relied on my own observations as well as many different sources for this book, and I have done my best to check facts and give credit where it is due. In the event that any material is used without proper permission, please contact me so that the oversight can be corrected.

The information provided in this book is for informational purposes only and is not intended to be a source of advice or credit analysis with respect to the material presented. The information and/or documents contained in this book do not constitute legal or financial advice and should never be used without first consulting with a financial professional to determine what may be best for your individual needs.

The publisher and the author do not make any guarantee or other promise as to any results that may be obtained from using the content of this book. You should never make any investment decision without first consulting with your own financial advisor and conducting your own research and due diligence. To the maximum extent permitted by law, the publisher and the author disclaim any and all liability in the event any information, commentary, analysis, opinions, advice, and/or recommendations contained in this book prove to be inaccurate, incomplete, or unreliable or result in any investment or other losses.

Content contained or made available through this book is not intended to and does not constitute legal advice or investment advice, and no attorney-client relationship is formed. The publisher and the author are providing this book and its contents on an "as is" basis. Your use of the information in this book is at your own risk.

TABLE OF CONTENTS.

TABLE OF CONTENTS. 4

INTRODUCTION 6

CHAPTER 1: UNDERSTANDING VALUE. 10

CHAPTER 2: CREATING VALUE FOR YOUR CUSTOMER. 27

CHAPTER 3: IMPORTANCE OF VALUE CREATION. 33

CHAPTER 4: VALUE CREATION STRUCTURE. 41

CHAPTER 5: VALUE CREATION EVALUATION. 49

CHAPTER 6: SALES VALUE AND HOW IT AFFECTS YOUR PRODUCT. 60

CHAPTER 7: CREATING IRRESISTIBLE OFFERS THAT IMMEDIATE PROMPT ACTION IS ADDED VALUE. 65

CHAPTER 8: HOW TO TRACK CUSTOMER VALUE OVER TIME. 70

CHAPTER 9: UNIQUE SELLING PROPOSITIONS FOR YOUR BUSINESS IN DIFFICULT TIMES. 79

CHAPTER 10: HOW TO BOOST YOUR CUSTOMERS' PERCEPTION OF YOUR VALUE. 88

CHAPTER 11: PROMOTING ON "LOW PRICE" BUT "VALUE" IS ESSENTIAL FOR SUCCESS. 94

CHAPTER 12: HOW A WEBSITE CAN INCREASE A COMPANY'S VALUE. 101

CHAPTER 13: STRATEGY AND CUSTOMER FOCUS. 105

CHAPTER 14: WAYS YOU CAN IMPROVE YOUR CUSTOMERS' EXPERIENCE. 112

CHAPTER 15: TIPS FOR ADDING EXTRA VALUE FOR YOUR CUSTOMERS..118

CONCLUSION. 123

INTRODUCTION.

Customers are something that you should never lose when conducting business. Without them, there would be no enterprise. You must do everything possible to establish and maintain a pleasant relationship with them.

Many things can be done to make this a reality, but many things can't be done to achieve the same result. Among all these issues, surplus value is the most important.

One of the worst mistakes that 99 percent of businesses make is allowing prospects and customers to come and go without considering how valuable they are to the future security of the company. Before you can get this answer, you must determine your customer's worth.

Every customer will purchase. How often during the year? How long? If you don't calculate these numbers, you have no business since you lack a significant asset. Your business lacks value. It may have cash flow, and you can have some money, but it is primarily a short-term investment.

You must always consider what you can do for your customers. If you possess any greed, it should be on behalf of your consumer. You desire to combat the avarice of your customers.

What advantages and benefits can you add to your product or service to make it irresistible?

Take out some paper and write the words down: "I can offer my customers" and "I can provide my customers more or less of what? I can provide my customers with improved what? I can provide my customers with stronger what? I can provide my customers with lesser or greater what?" Anything more you can conceive of offering your customers.

Then, compare your current talents and capabilities with the enumerated other benefits and features and calculate what it may cost to supply these services. Include the new features and benefits, the additional cost, and a breakdown of the cost's components. Such is the cost of the product, shipping, fulfillment, labor, inventory, and storage. All these factors are considered when performing an exercise of this nature.

If you operate a service-based business, express the other cost regarding the time required to deliver the added feature or benefit. This extra time should be compared to the time spent working for someone else, eight hours per day, five days per week, against the time spent studying how to produce money in your business.

You can work smarter by understanding how to make your money work hard for you as you do by making your product or service work harder for you than you do. You can accomplish far more with less effort.

If you treat everyone as a VIP, they will build your business for you. You will provide the necessary time and service to maintain good customer relations. Similarly, you might spend less time acquiring new customers with a service firm if you treat your current customers differently.

Remember that while marketing may be undertaken for the public, your customers will concentrate on one thing at a time. Even though you are marketing to the entire market, you must treat your customers as unique individuals.

CHAPTER 1: UNDERSTANDING VALUE.

What Is Value?

Profit is the difference between your costs and the price you receive in the marketplace for anything. Profitability depends on value. Understanding value may provide a wealth of information about how to increase profits in any firm. A useful method to consider this is:

Price - Cost = Profit.

This implies that large earnings are always the result of a thorough understanding of expenses and pricing, although this can be considerably more challenging than it sounds.

Profit can be viewed differently, but it is essential to understand profit's role in capitalist society to grasp the concept fully. In a free market, the objective of profit is to draw people and capital to activities that benefit others. This suggests that most organizations with profitability concerns are most likely dealing with one of the following issues:

1) Costing.

2) Getting customers.

3) Controlling cost.

4) Producing value.

Many businesspeople become fixated on the concept of cost control, which receives considerably more attention than merits. In most sectors, the cost isn't the most essential consideration in the customer's purchasing choice, despite its importance. People tend to focus on cost reduction since it is simple. This is the incorrect approach if you want to generate enormous riches.

The key to astronomical profits.

As you can have predicted from the preceding sentence, insane profits are just the result of providing immense value to a group of wealthy consumers. In addition, that last point regarding spending money is essential.

I know individuals who have constructed ambitious business plans for customers with little to no disposable income, failing due to a lack of funds. Remember what Willie Sutton said when asked why bank robbers commit crimes:

Since that is where the money is

Creating value can be simple, or it can be challenging. Many people are capable of simple value creation. However, very few will engage in challenging or intricate value creation. You will earn more money if you know how to charge for challenging tasks. This is important since you must understand the implications of competition. Consider the following:

What is the value of a glass of water?

A glass of water isn't all that valuable to you if you are now seated at home or in your workplace. Perhaps a nickel on the exterior. Why? Because you can easily walk over to a tap and fill a glass with water for less than a nickel without spending much time or having an extensive understanding of water.

If I were standing next to you with the sole glass of water for 100 miles, you would esteem that drink significantly more. Consider, on the other hand, the value of that water if you were involved in a plane accident in the desert. The alternative would not exist, yet the water demand would certainly exist. This leads to an essential concept regarding value:

Your accessible alternatives define value.

In other words, if there is an easily accessible alternative to a product or service, most buyers will value it similarly. This is one of the reasons why banks and airlines typically offer fairly similar interest rates and tickets. Why would you pay more for one if there is no discernible difference between the options?

This is where competition enters the picture.

When you do something simple that generates value, a rival can do the same thing and may even do it for a nickel less to acquire the consumer. Almost always, rivals' willingness to reduce prices is constrained by their costs. This means that most of your competitors will reduce their rates to the point where they lose money on the transaction to steal customers from you.

Of course, if you look at it from a different perspective, they are sacrificing earnings for customers. Still, most industry competitors will do this, believing that volume sales will compensate for the loss. Consider a lemonade stand to comprehend the reality of this issue.

Suppose you run a lemonade stand and your cost per glass of lemonade is 20 cents due to using lemonade mix, cups, and other supplies. You decide to price 50 cents a glass your delicious lemonade, resulting in the following profit scenario:

Price=$0.50 - Cost=$0.20.

Profit=$0.30.

To determine the entire profit of a business with multiple sales, we must add the revenue and expenses for each transaction. A useful method to consider this is:

Sales=Units X Price.

The "unit" for lemonade is a glass of lemonade, so:

Sales = Lemonade Glasses X Price.

Let's assume that 100 customers purchase lemonade daily in this neighborhood. Yes, my childhood neighborhood was never that great, but we are pretending, so bear with me. This results in the following overall profit picture:

Sales=$50.00 - Cost=$20.00.

Profit=$30.00.

Suppose that one day, Egbert puts up a stand beside yours. Let's imagine you both run to the corner store to get lemonade mix, which costs approximately 20 cents per serving and has identical costs. When you launch your lemonade stand, your profit potential may appear as follows:

Price=$0.50 – Cost=$0.20.

Profit=$0.30.

Egbert is naturally nasty as a rival and can't stand the concept of you getting money. Therefore, Egbert chooses to steal your customers by reducing his pricing. Customers, being who they are, will occasionally transfer to a lower-priced alternative, although others won't. Suppose Egbert is satisfied with this profit picture.

Price=$0.40 - Cost=$0.20.

Profit=$0.20.

This will almost surely cause you to lose consumers to Egbert. Who could blame them? The buyer receives the identical lemonade for 10 cents less - what a deal! Now comes the tough part: some customers won't switch and will continue to purchase from you.

Why? I've given up trying to comprehend, but it's entirely accurate. Given the option, some individuals will still pay more than the lowest price available. Perhaps your eyes appeal to them, or they are unwilling to take the extra five steps to reach Egbert's booth.

Why bother? You retain these customers despite charging a higher price. Sounds good, right? It is. All else being equal, most customers will purchase from Egbert, say 80 of them. You retain 20 customers owing to your charisma, amusing sales banter, and good location. This results in the following overall profit picture:

Sales=$10.00 - Cost=$4.00.

Profit=$6.00.

While Egbert's overall profit picture seems as follows:

Sales=$32.00 -Cost=$16.00.

Profit=$16.00.

Egbert is earning more money than you. Since evil never triumphs, you desire to regain some of those customers. You reduced your pricing to $0.40 to match Egbert's. What occurs? You and Egbert will likely split the market evenly, with 50 customers each. This leaves both of you with the following profit picture:

Sales=$20.00 −Cost=$10.00.

Profit=$10.00.

Consider what has transpired here. When you started selling lemonade, you were earning $30.00 each day. Egbert arrived and reduced your daily profits to $6, so he could earn $16 each day, and as a result of matching his price, you ended up earning $10.00 every day.

In this example, the total profit made by ALL lemonade vendors in your neighborhood decreased from $30.00 (when you were the only one selling) to $22.00 (after Egbert entered the market and lowered pricing) to $20.00 (when you were both priced the same and made the same profit). The lemonade and the consumers remained the same, so what consumed the profit?

Profit is eroded by competition.

A. Developing Worth.

The creation of value is among the most significant aspects of profitability. If you visit a grocery shop and purchase an item (such as a box of dog treats), you won't be able to stand outside the store and resell the item for a higher price.

This is because the box of dog treats sold outside the business isn't much more or less valuable than the same box offered inside. You compete with the store by selling identical things in a neighboring area. But more fundamentally, you have not created any value.

Your box of dog treats has the same value to the customer as the one at the store. Most customers will only pay more for your dog treats than they would in a store if you provide other value. Here are a few things that could improve the value of your dog treats:

You remove them from the package and feed them to the dog.

You improve them by adding sugar to them.

You place them in a box that is more aesthetically pleasing.

Customers feel good about purchasing from you.

You embrace the buyer for purchasing from you.

You perform while selling dog treats.

Hopefully, you will grasp the concept. You can add value by improving the product, changing the packaging, or doing anything else that enhances the customer's overall purchasing experience—possibly not a lot of value, perhaps only a cent or two for each treat. However, if you sell enough sweets, this might add up, and you will undoubtedly have a greater ability to profit from your products than your competitors.

B. Achieving Uniqueness.

The competitive circumstance with Egbert we discussed isn't all that uncommon. Unless you do something competitors can't replicate, you will have competition, even if it isn't particularly strong.

How do you make your profit picture appear as if you had no competitors?

The idea is to discover a method to be distinctive. Idealistically, you want to find a uniqueness that some of your customers find important. Still, even plain strangeness and oddness might count for something - just examine the success of Ben & Jerry's and the Rainforest Café.

In a vanilla world, chocolate will command a premium price. Remember, though, that if your uniqueness is successful and generates a profitable company, your competitors will likely attempt to imitate it sooner or later.

Uniqueness provides a competitive advantage, which may be maintained by making it extremely difficult for competitors to imitate you. There are many ways to accomplish this. Competitors will fail at copying if one of the following occurs:

1. They can't copy your originality.

2. They opt not to copy your singularity.

3. They can't duplicate your distinctiveness.

4. The opponent replicates you ineffectively because they lack concentration.

Let's examine how to keep originality in light of these four elements.

Competitors will replicate differentiating qualities that are extremely tough to replicate or need difficult-to-acquire talents. To utilize this element, select distinctions that necessitate expertise that you possess but your competitors lack.

It is extremely difficult to persuade a competitor to do anything. To prevent competitors from copying your differentiation, you can wish to select one that is superficially unappealing. For instance, any differentiator that increases prices or contradicts traditional thinking regarding how people make money in your sector may be deemed "impractical" by your competitors.

I've worked with firms that made millions by focusing on the least desirable customers in their industry simply because their competitors didn't take the time to determine why no one wanted those customers.

There are few ways to prohibit a competitor from copying you; most require legal and/or governmental assistance. Patent protection is an excellent illustration of this, as it is a practical means for preserving originality.

Unfortunately, most of these strategies have a finite lifespan. Thus, you should increase your distinctiveness in some other way while under government protection. If you don't, you'll discover that reliance on legal protection may be a crippling addiction, and quitting cold turkey is often fatal.

The focus advantage is undoubtedly one of the simplest and simplest instruments available to smaller businesses. It is especially important when competing with much larger enterprises.

If you focus on a niche market substantially narrower than your larger competition, you will likely become the niche's favored provider. As a result of concentrating your efforts on satisfying the wants of a specific sort of consumer, you should be able to generate a significantly bigger profit.

Many smaller businesses reject this strategy because they believe it restricts their growth potential. However, the contrary is typically true. In the insurance industry, for instance, we have observed companies earn tremendous profitability and growth by targeting a market that is less than 5 percent of the market their competitors have targeted.

Too many individuals view profit as a basic, black-and-white concept that can only be addressed through predictable, replicable means, such as cost reduction. Understanding how uniqueness leads to profit is a fantastic strategy to differentiate your firm and achieve above-average profitability. You can distinguish your business and properly position your firm for long-term competitive advantage in the market with a little effort.

CHAPTER 2: CREATING VALUE FOR YOUR CUSTOMER.

From a service provider's perspective, acquiring a new customer is important in the global marketplace. This cycle of acquiring a customer is typically lengthy, not only because of contractual and legal implications but also because customers often base work-awarding decisions on "what value the organization will gain" by bringing in the service provider (or vendor) to the organization.

Working with newly acquired customers or existing customers is proving extremely difficult for the service provider community in the current business environment due to economic slowdown, ramp-down business, stiff competition, pricing impact and increased cost of operation and maintenance, etc. Consequently, they are compelled to seek improved services at a lower price.

On the other hand, once the business is acquired, the service provider tends to become somewhat complacent with the belief that the customer will remain and that the business can be managed as it comes. Relationships between the customer and service provider can become strained if the focus on building relationships isn't conducted positively. This can lead to the development of cracks.

Today's customers view service providers as business partners and are willing to share their business eco-system to help the service provider comprehend how they conduct business. It should appear to be a business marriage and a strengthening of each other's core competencies instead of a one-time partnership.

Customers are increasingly interested in developing long-term relationships with their service providers and establishing a common platform for exchanging business requirements for a shared objective.

The modern service provider must focus on enhancing the customer's business experience for his organization, customers, and competitors. What type of service, product, or tool proposition and implementation can give the customer a competitive advantage over his rivals?

From the customer's perspective, his state of mind consists of how drastically he can increase his bottom line or top line and how he can increase his customer base and revenue targets, or how he can minimize the operational, technical, or service-related issues that are impacting the business or how he can reduce the operation and maintenance costs of his IT services.

Most professionally managed global organizations that engage in vendor management and outsource their products or services or both have short-, medium- and long-term business plans to derive significant business benefits from service providers and measure them as part of a BLA, SLA, or OLA.

These agreements are typically well-designed at the outset of a contractual relationship and regularly reviewed with the service provider.

The services of service providers (vendors) are no longer justified based on the amount of money paid to them per hour and their ability to demonstrate, following contractual terms, what has been accomplished to receive payment. In terms of value ads, customers expect much more cream than just a dollar's worth as a freebie.

Customers anticipate that service providers will have multiple positive effects on their businesses. Therefore, it is imperative that service providers plan for it and continuously demonstrate the value they are creating for their customers.

It became essential for service providers to develop value-added proposals for the customer's business growth and to plan for the customer's capability demonstration to demonstrate greater confidence.

For a service provider, the experience with a newly acquired customer should be analogous to a sporting event in which the first few minutes are essential. If you demonstrate a professional game with a winning attitude and confidence in achieving results, your chances of gaining a new customer are very good. Also, even being an experienced player, you must win every game to establish credibility.

Today's service providers must adhere to the maxim "Win the customer every day." Every small action taken by the service provider must result in the desired outcome for the customer. It necessitates interacting with the customer from a business-centric perspective and managing the customer experience with greater rigor.

A couple of surveys conducted by service providers may indicate a higher proportion of customer-centric strategies, but the reality is that only a fraction of customers will agree.

Session highlight: As a service provider in a game-changing business environment, it is essential to adapt to your customer's business environment and quickly align yourself to demonstrate that the customer's changing goals are your goals going forward.

For instance, if the customer desires a 10% reduction in overall costs, what will your service provider proposal be for optimizing and consolidating services? You must make your customer feel like you are integral to his mission.

CHAPTER 3: IMPORTANCE OF VALUE CREATION.

In engineering terminology, the concept of a "perpetual motion machine" operates on producing more output than inputs; similarly, the business community expects greater production per dollar spent.

1. Customer organizations feel the need for value creation globally for different reasons.

2. Customers seek differentiators that can positively impact their business outcomes.

3. As part of their business philosophy, businesses tend to get more with less expenditure.

4. Market pressure, fierce competition, business complexities, and growth trajectories exert intense pressure on them to do more with less.

5. To ensure their survival, managers from customer organizations must impress their management by acquiring these other benefits from their service providers.

6. It is possible to compare and select service providers based on the added value they provide to the business.

7. The customer expects the service provider to be a growth partner.

What is the value creation process?

By intent, the definition of value creation could be different for each customer based on his business objectives and pain points; however, in a simplified sense, it could be the act of a service provider that satisfies a customer (during the creation, implementation or management of a service or product) by providing returns above the customer's investments or the cost of the services.

As a contractual requirement, it is sometimes referred to as a freebie because it comes free with the service or product rendered.

Differentiating value creation from paid services:

There is perpetual confusion among many professionals regarding the distinction between value creation and paid services.

For example, a customer organization may be unsurprised if you deliver services and or products following contractual payment terms and conditions; however, the value created for the same customer may exceed the dollar value paid and be expressed in terms of tangible or intangible benefits such as return on investment, improved customer satisfaction in the customer organization, reduction in the overall number of business issues or problems, or an increase in customer base.

Value creation details are not quantified in contractual terms in the statement of work or purchase order but are de facto and often unwritten customer expectations. In some cases, the service provider must uncover them and bring them to the attention of customer stakeholders to earn their trust.

Value creation has a long-lasting impact on the overall business climate of the customer's organization.

Strategy for creating value:

Why employ strategy?

Due to the explosion in demand for IT services, service provider organizations have recently begun stating in their core principles of working toward the customer that they believe in developing a business strategy to deliver greater value. These strategies can improve the customer's confidence by aligning with his business objectives or concerns and providing reassurance.

In a sense, creating value for a customer is an ongoing process that must be revised as the customer's business objectives or concerns change in response to his business environment.

Session highlight: The business strategy that a service provider must develop for his customer must create at least two times the size of the contract value he receives from the customer.

Different levels of value creation:

Customer value creation occurs in many ways and requires a comprehensive understanding of the customer's stakeholders, business, technology, and operations. Customer Organization's stakeholders include personnel, senior management, end users, customers, and other vendors.

Depending on their problems, issues, concerns, and business objectives, the value perceived by each individual may vary. The service provider must consider all these factors when providing services to an organization.

The value created by the service provider varies in flavor and is contingent on the circumstances. It is an ongoing process that is created at the instance level. It can be roughly categorized into two levels for convenience's sake.

Strategic or Business Level: At the business level, value creation is the aggregated effect on the business environment as a result of the service or product provided by the service provider and is quantified in terms of numbers, percentages, factors, etc. Calculating and determining business value is difficult and can occasionally be misleading. Often is, the valuation of value creation intangible.

Good examples of a service provider's tangible value creation are the number of new customers acquired by the customer due to the service provider's exceptional performance and the percentage or dollar amount of revenue growth.

Intangible values are difficult to quantify; therefore, they could be described as the service provider's ability to assist the customer in consistently implementing the regulatory standard, maintaining compliance, providing ease of operation, or sourcing difficult skills when the business urgently requires them.

At the operation level, value creation may be tangible or intangible, depending on the customer organization's business environment. Creating value at the operational level may or may not have a global impact on the business environment. It has a more local focus.

Examples of tangible value creation by a service provider include SLA-based improvements, high system availability, a reduction in downtime by a percentage, and an improvement in response time by a percentage. Intangible value measures include the highest level of collaboration, outstanding teamwork, and process compliance.

The value created for each customer organization stakeholder is broadly classified at the business and operation levels.

CHAPTER 4: VALUE CREATION STRUCTURE.

Every service provider must develop a customer-specific framework for value creation that is aligned with the customer's business environment and can be used continuously to generate value-added instances. The framework provides the service provider organization's team members with a lot of consistency and a distinct understanding.

Such a framework should function as a value-creation engine and be supported by tools and processes to continuously capture the customer's pulse. The service provider may need to invest in this area, considering the expansion of his business and customer relationship.

Understand value propositions and develop a strategy:

Typically, the value creation proposition begins on the first day of customer engagement. The service provider and his team must make a concerted effort to plan each activity that increases the customer's value methodically. When a customer submits a fresh service request, the provider must prioritize providing other value over low-cost services.

Often, a customer may not be clear or vocal about what can truly make a difference for his business; in such cases, the service provider must validate his understanding of the value his customer's organization could gain by completing specific tasks. This can be accomplished through various discussion forums and by examining the work scope.

Here are a few inputs that can aid in developing a structured plan for creating value.

1. Determine what the customer values in it;

2. Distinguish between the technology and business aspects of customer engagement;

3. Determine which features and services are of the utmost importance to the customer;

4. Identify the customer's greatest challenges, issues, constraints, or problems; and

5. Speak with stakeholders such as technical team leads, end users, customers, and senior management to comprehend business imperatives and impacts.

6. Understand the customer's environment, market, customers, location, industry, and culture. Understand how customer intimacy and collaboration can be improved.

7. Establish a shared understanding and definition of value with the customer.

Implement value creation plan:

Implementing the value creation plan within the service provider's organization requires concentration and consensus. Every resource engaged in providing services to the customer should have a clear understanding of the value that must be delivered to the customer over time and the method by which this information can be communicated to the management of both the customer organization and the service provider organization.

The value creation plan must consider some value add proposals at the technology, process, tool, or business level that can benefit the customer; each proposal must be evaluated in light of the customer's business environment.

The service provider organization must believe in an open culture of working with customers and dare to point out ambiguity, blind spots, and problem areas formally to minimize the negative impact on the customer's business.

Every element of a benefit that can add value to any stakeholder of the customer organization must be considered. Occasionally, value-added proposals may have both short-term and long-term benefits.

During the implementation of a value-added proposal, the focus should be on retaining valuable resources that can generate significant value for the customer organization.

Capture, qualify, and quantify instances of value creation:

Often, teams of a service provider's organization perform a lot of value-added work for their customer but fail to provide visibility to the customer and the management of the service provider's organization, so it goes unnoticed. This disadvantages the service provider team because it loses the chance to be recognized.

Another disadvantage is that the senior management of the service provider organization lacks perspective and therefore misses the chance to demonstrate best practices to other prospective customers. As a result, the value creation framework and its dissemination to the service provider organization's team provide the correct solution to this issue.

Value creation transforms the customer's business status in a way that makes him more competitive and enables him to meet his business objectives promptly.

The measurement of value creation necessitates implementing a systematic process to ensure that all instances of value addition are captured, quantified, represented, and approved by the customer.

This contributes to establishing a more convincing foundation for strengthening and cultivating the relationship. Typically, customers experience the effects of value-added services they have received from service providers.

Qualifying what constitutes a value-added service for a specific customer is essential, and this is accomplished through close collaboration and frequent consultation with customer organization representatives at all levels.

The focus of qualifying a value-added service comes from the customer's business environment, and it is essential to identify bottlenecks, obstacles, and issues through continuous dialogue, review meetings, and management presentations.

Once the attributes of qualifying value elements have been determined, a process and/or tools can be designed to capture, quantify and measure them at the desired frequency. It is also essential to verify the eligibility requirements with the customer.

For instance, if a customer faces change management issues with his staff when implementing a new business process through an IT system and you are an IT system service provider, you can offer him a change facilitator who can effectively address this issue to prevent deployment failures. Consequently, the qualification of what will truly be of value to the customer is paramount.

Quantification occurs immediately following the determination of the customer's qualified value.

Quantifying a value-added element from its nonexistent or minimal state to its tangible form after you, as a service provider, have worked on it can demonstrate your success. Whether a customer or a service provider, quantifying value addition in measurable terms always provides a comparative reference indicator within the organization and, often, among competitors.

This value quantification is accomplished in many ways, such as with numbers, percentages, or on a scale of 0 to 5 or 0 to 10. Accurate calculation of value-added measures promptly and at a logical periodicity provides a good trend to help the service provider achieve more while showcasing this trend at periodic intervals increases the customer's confidence.

CHAPTER 5: VALUE CREATION EVALUATION.

Measuring value creation requires a clear understanding and definition of measures, timely capture, and convincing communication with the customer.

Value creation occurs differently and continues until the service provider begins working with the customer organization. These metrics should also measure the performance of tools, processes, and people to determine whether they produce value-based outcomes.

Listed below are some typical metrics that prove that value creation is occurring.

Customer Delight Index (CDI): This is one of the measures that service providers can use to determine the level of customer satisfaction. This metric can be collected at regular intervals.

The rising trend in CDI and its consistent maintenance at the highest level indicates that the customer is pleased with the quality of your services. One can determine which aspects of services contribute the most to customer satisfaction.

A few examples of customer satisfaction include timely delivery of services throughout an engagement or period, demonstrating service level performance that exceeds the agreed-upon SLA, and question response times that are significantly faster than the agreed-upon timeline.

Utilizing innovative techniques and concepts while providing services to a customer can improve throughput by decreasing system downtime.

For instance, if you are responsible for the maintenance of customers' IT systems, which used to experience four to six hours of downtime per week, and you have created innovatively better maintenance procedures and tools to reduce such downtime to just one or two hours drastically, you can be eligible for a bonus. This is an excellent example of added value to showcase to your customer.

After capturing the value-added metrics, it is necessary to represent them in the appropriate forum. Service providers can share the results of their efforts to create value-added services with customer organizations during periodic management, business, and progress reviews.

To create a conducive environment and demonstrate that they are aligned with the business objectives or concerns of the customer organization, service providers often choose contract renewal or extension periods to discuss value additions with customers.

Such value-added services are shared with the customer at the team level through case studies or best practices. One of the essential aspects of determining whether or not we have created value for our customers can be addressed by getting an external perspective. You can get this perspective by speaking with an analyst group, a competitor, or a surveying organization.

This is somewhat complicated due to confidentiality concerns and, at times, the ambiguity of value-added measures. Service providers can utilize a third-party perspective to comprehend the value creation for large customer organizations.

Judging the customer's pulse and his endorsement of value creation for the work performed by the service provider also indicates whether or not the stakeholders in the customer organization are satisfied and whether or not the relationship is a win-win.

Session highlights include:

Value creation framework is a long-term asset for the customer organization that gives him confidence and visibility into what the service provider can do to increase his business value.

Tools for value creation: Service provider organizations may have created and implemented specific tools for multiple customers, some of which may be identical for similar engagements. Depending on the customer's business environment, it may be necessary to develop tools that, if used effectively, can provide greater benefits and value to the customer.

Considering those tools that can yield quick results for the customer organization is essential. This must be done before the customer believes he is no longer receiving value from the service provider.

The following are examples of recommended tools:

Many service providers invariably use return on Investment (ROI) models to demonstrate the value accruing from engagements over time. Choosing the parameters for input and output makes ROI calculations challenging.

1. Reusable components: This is one of the greatest assets a service provider can capitalize on, as reusable components can have a positive impact on

the deliverables and output of the service provider's organization, thereby reducing errors, saving time, and providing a head start for customer engagements.

If a service provider does not already have reusable components, he can create them for his customer so that the customer organization can utilize them without other time and effort. It becomes an asset that adds value.

In addition, calculating and demonstrating the value-added service or product to a customer organization that uses it regularly is relatively simple. Sets of requirement/use cases, test cases, templates, objects, and platforms are typical examples of reusable components, as are standard business process flows for a particular business process or product.

2. Customer satisfaction survey: A customer satisfaction survey is one of the most effective methods utilized by nearly every service provider to gauge the level of value-added services provided to the customer.

Many service provider businesses have built survey portals for their customers to collect feedback on their value-added services to various stakeholders. The survey responses include specific questions and scores describing the value-added service/product service providers provided.

3. Idea generation and innovation models: This is one of the top and most popular expectations that customer organizations have of their service providers, and renewal contracts often examine these aspects in great detail.

The customer organization wants to know what framework the service provider has developed, what components are demonstrable, and whether or not the resources consider every problem and issue creatively, etc. In reality, the origins of value-added services stem entirely from new solutions.

Many service provider organizations have portals, frameworks, and initiatives for fostering employee-generated innovation and ideas that can be implemented to provide value-added services to their customers.

4. Value register: Maintaining a value register and recording all instances of value-added services provided to the customer promptly is a straightforward approach to capturing all instances of value added for the customer throughout the engagements.

5. Motivational tools: Many service provider organizations use motivational tools with incentives, rewards, etc., to encourage the generation of new, creative, and innovative ideas.

Often, customer organizations also present certificates and monetary rewards to service provider workers in recognition of their exceptional contributions and value-added services. Examples include providing out-of-the-box solutions to customer issues or problems that are not typical of day-to-day operations.

6. Utilizing best practices are comparable to employing reusable components. As a result of the fact that many service providers work in multiple customer environments, the best practices collected from other customer accounts and engagements are stored in a repository and applied when similar situations for other customers arise.

Using best practices to address customer issues or problems is highly effective when the corporate environment and circumstances are identical. This adds significant value to the customer's organization.

7. Customer-specific instruments: Relationship management and visibility at the management level are of the utmost importance in larger customer accounts. Most service providers make an effort to create program dashboards, scorecards, SLA management dashboards, and reporting portals to display the accomplishments, progress trends on various metrics, and the overall account health. This service provides value to the customer organization.

8. Tools for escalations and problem management: These are fairly common yet essential tools, especially for large customer accounts. The clear added benefit of such solutions to the customer is a large decrease in the time and effort required to process escalated issues and escalations.

When it negatively influences the business, it is essential to share information with the necessary parties, such as when problems arise or escalate, who is addressing them, and what the resolution is. With these tools, you can design an excellent workflow and end-to-end process.

Many service provider businesses populate the issue and escalation databases for future problem management. Even for smaller customer accounts, a simple Excel-based issue/escalations register with the necessary facts provides a solid repository, and such previous events might be helpful for future issues of a similar sort.

9. Six sigma tools: Six sigma tools are highly effective and focused on results. They aid service

provider teams in capturing the Voice of the Customer (VOC) at the definition phase. Critical to Quality (CTQ) measures are identified and tracked throughout the improvement cycle.

Six sigma tools are enough to demonstrate value, as six sigma projects normally take two to three months to complete. Since the technology is widely used and accepted, it is simple to persuade customers of the benefits of using it to demonstrate value additions.

Session highlights include: Tools are the resources that continually enable service providers to perform better for their customers at a lower cost.

In conclusion, creating value for your customer isn't a one-time exercise aimed at putting a smile on his face but a continuous process of implementing a business strategy supported by innovative solutions and managing it throughout the customer engagement to demonstrate measurable 2x returns on his investments.

CHAPTER 6: SALES VALUE AND HOW IT AFFECTS YOUR PRODUCT.

The consumer mostly determines the definition of what provides value. You either do what is best for the consumer (as previously established) or don't. From the consumer's perspective, "value-added" implies nothing. It does not add significant value to the product itself. The product's base value will have to stand on its own.

Consumers will purchase from a sales representative who genuinely cares about their needs and isn't offering "extra" items to make the sale.

I have spent years attempting to convince sales representatives that the value they "bring" originates from themselves. It isn't something the corporation offers to compensate for their inability to comprehend the consumer and his/her wants.

Claiming to offer a value-added service is like telling a potential customer, "Buy this car from me because the tires are inflated."

Giving Value initially necessitates adopting the perspective of the buyer. Understand that the buyer is always attempting to meet his or her desires and requirements, never yours. You are not being considered! It is always about them and never about you.

Four levels of buyer contentment:

You must meet the expectations of the consumer. Consider how you can accomplish this with your product or service. Understand that the product or service satisfies a customer's demands, not any added value. Nothing added to the goods or services can help you achieve customer expectations.

I'm not suggesting that the extras are unimportant; they're the subject of the following statement. I mean that the product carries certain expectations, which must be met, or the buyer will search elsewhere. The expectations are focused on the product, not your value addition.

Can you provide a list of twenty probable buyer expectations before your first conversation?

Can you demonstrate how your product meets these requirements without using superlatives? Create a list of twenty items that will satisfy the buyer's requirements. The following day, add twenty more items to the list.

Once the prospective buyer is convinced you can meet his expectations, you must demonstrate your ability to exceed them. You must continuously question how you might exceed the expectations of potential buyers - by adding what to the initial purchase product.

Here is where you provide value additions.

Consider twenty ways in which you can exceed the expectations of your prospective buyers. Consider these factors from the perspective of your new customers to see if you are on target. If not, return and generate twenty more ideas. The following day, add twenty more items to the list.

Next, you must continue to please the customer after the moment of sale. Sometimes referred to as "sales satisfaction." You must comprehend the distinction between satisfaction and pleasure. Ask yourself continually, "How can I delight my customer? He then devises means to achieve customer satisfaction. Can you come up with twenty methods to please your customers?

Will you consider twenty extra words tomorrow?

How do you intend to implement today's changes?

What are your plans for the next day?

You know that impressing the potential buyer at each stage of the sales process is essential to being the best. Ultimately, you must comprehend the power of awe. Stop right now and consider twenty ways you might astonish your potential buyer from the initial contact until he refers you to his friends. The following day, consider twenty more. Plan how you want to apply these measures.

Value necessitates that you comprehend your buyer! Your product is your value, and your product is yours. Without you, your product is nothing more than a commodity. Professionals in sales take the commodity, add themselves to the mix and generate tremendous value for prospective purchasers.

CHAPTER 7: CREATING IRRESISTIBLE OFFERS THAT IMMEDIATE PROMPT ACTION IS ADDED VALUE.

Adding value involves providing customers with more than they could receive elsewhere. Most individuals today are value-driven. It's not the price that matters most; the added value they receive justifies the cost of your widget.

Offer significantly more use value to your customers than you get in financial worth. When you offer more with every purchase, buyers perceive that purchase as having greater value. This added value gives you a clear and unmistakable competitive advantage over all other businesses selling comparable products.

The objective here is to increase the value of whatever you are selling. Make it far more advantageous and valuable for the buyer to purchase from you. You want the buying decision to be a "no-brainer" in your favor due to the substantial added value you provide.

Including other bonuses with each purchase is a simple way to improve value. This could entail including a lovely bag with each laptop, an apron with each pasta maker, or a high-quality tool belt with each power drill. Many such rewards are available from specialized vendors in bulk and at affordable costs.

Providing free printed reports, audiotapes, films, or CDs is a simple and inexpensive method to offer value. The goal is to deliver timely and useful information to the buyer. Hopefully, it is also something he or she can't discover elsewhere.

Often, these "extras" can be replicated at a very cheap cost, but the perceived value they offer to a product can be worth a hundred times or more than their real costs.

A substantial component of effective writing is a compelling offer. The more compelling your offer is to potential customers, the greater your likelihood of closing the deal. Many direct response specialists accord that if you want to increase your results, you must improve your offer. A better offer means greater value. Buyers receive greater value for their money.

There are many good examples of value-added marketing displayed on television. You can turn on the television anytime or at night and witness many examples of other values.

Using this singular premise, the Ginsu Knife has been sold commercially for years. You receive multiple knives for one low price. "Buy the world-famous Ginsu Deluxe, and you'll also receive this and this, and if you order within the next eight minutes, you'll also receive this unique extra item for free!" The Ginsu brand's marketers have sold millions of packages utilizing this value-added strategy.

Observe any infomercial on television today, and you will see that the same added value offers are consistently employed. Why? Because they function exceptionally well.

Book and CD clubs utilize the concept of added value to acquire a portion of this valuable market. How can they attract people accustomed to purchasing books and CDs at the local mall? By providing exceptional value upfront. "5 Books For $5" or "Choose Any 3 CDs FREE With Your First Order" are examples of improved value offers given primarily to attract first-time consumers.

Almost any organization might provide value with simple information products. Create things with added value and "inside information" that benefit your customers. It may be how to get more out of their new equipment, how to maintain it so it lasts longer and performs reliably for years, or how to utilize your new widget 37 different ways around the house or office.

Another alternative is to provide buyers with the information they are likely to find valuable. For instance, a strawberry farm could provide one or two fantastic recipes for strawberry shortcakes, pies, or tarts. It isn't difficult to create the perception of added value. This is a basic, affordable, and appropriate value-added example.

Providing extra value creates a situation where all parties are satisfied with the acquisition. Your consumers receive more value for their money and are delighted to share their positive experiences with others. The addition of value increases referral business. As word spreads about the unique benefits that your firm offers, you get a larger consumer base.

How can you improve the perceived value of your current offer? A small amount of inventiveness can make your sales offering considerably more appealing, and an enticing offer attracts many more interested customers.

CHAPTER 8: HOW TO TRACK CUSTOMER VALUE OVER TIME.

The holy grail of online marketing is tracking lifetime customer value and assessing the ROI of each of your marketing vehicles. Unfortunately, many online marketers lack the execution skills necessary to realize this ambition. These marketers get the objective of assessing lifetime customer value but use so many shortcuts that their conclusions are dubious.

Tracking lifetime customer value is more difficult than it initially appears since marketers rely on two distinct systems for customer tracking, and these systems typically don't communicate with one another. The first tracking system is a web analytics package, the most popular of which is Google Analytics.

The second tracking system is the transactional system (such as an e-commerce database) that records customers and orders. Although the online analytics package has information about where customers originated, customer lifetime value is typically stored in the transactional system, posing a barrier.

Because marketers don't comprehend how to interface their analytics software with their transactional system, they begin to take shortcuts. The most frequent shortcut is to get an average lifetime customer value from the transactional system and presume that value applies to all customer categories.

This significant assumption often fails to hold water when you can access genuine customer lifetime value by segment. The reality is that certain parts spend significantly more than others. Therefore, you must look deeper.

On occasion, marketers estimate customer value based on the information in Ad Words or Google Analytics (when the e-commerce capabilities are turned on.) The issue with this strategy is that Ad Words employs a 30-day cookie, so you can only track consumer expenditure for the first 30 days after a user clicks on an ad. That is an insufficient amount of time to gauge lifetime value.

There are two fundamental methods for effectively tracking lifetime customer value: transfer customer source information to your transactional system or extract sufficient information from your analytics package to match it with your transactional system. In the first case, you tag each sponsored advertising campaign with other data that defines a customer's origin.

For example, suppose we are running advertisements for your website. Instead of putting "http://YourURLHere.com/" for the landing page when configuring the advertisements, we use "http://YourURLHere.com/?source=123," where 123 represents the ad campaign.

The transactional system must then capture "?source=123" and associate this data with the correct customer. In other words, when a consumer clicks on the ad, you store "123" in your database column for that customer.

If you created your transactional system, this modification is typically not difficult on most platforms. Depending on the flexibility of your packaged transactional/e-commerce system, this strategy may or may not be applicable.

In addition to the integration challenges, this strategy has other advantages and disadvantages. Once this system is operational, it is rather simple to generate reports detailing the overall income by campaign and what customers purchased and when. This is because all segmentation and revenue data resides in a single location: your transactional systems.

However, you don't have the cost of your campaigns in the transactional systems, so you will still need to match them up. However, this is typically a straightforward task that can be completed manually if you don't have many campaigns.

This strategy works for sponsored advertising campaigns and other strategies where you can control the URL (to append "?source=123" information). In certain circumstances, such as free search, you can't control the URL.

Consequently, you can't calculate ROI for all sources using this method. While we are primarily interested in the ROI of paid advertising campaigns, it is always beneficial to know the ROI of SEO work and other marketing projects.

The second method for tracking lifetime customer value is to collect sufficient data from the web analytics system to determine where customers originated. If you are utilizing Google Analytics, you must activate the e-commerce features.

After completing these steps, you can generate reports in Google Analytics that display transaction IDs by customer source. For instance, one can select the E-Commerce area, and the Transactions report in

Google Analytics. You can then choose a segment or utilize the secondary dimension to filter the results.

You now have a list of transactions organized by their source. This information may be exported from Google and imported into a reporting database for your transactional system, where you can view the subsequent purchases made by customers from each source.

In other words, Google Analytics informs you that order 1001 was placed by a consumer who arrived from a certain campaign. You can now access your transactional system to determine that this customer subsequently placed orders 1010 and 1011.

To export data from Google Analytics, it is advisable to utilize an automated program. Excellent Analytics is an Excel add-in that utilizes the Google Analytics API to retrieve data from Google Analytics. This strategy requires some effort to set up, but it is incredibly beneficial if you pursue it.

This second method applies to nearly all customer sources, which is one of its many benefits. Want to know how much money organic search customers spend?

There are no issues with this method. You can make the data as granular as you desire.

For instance, you can determine the lifetime value of users who arrived at a given keyword phrase via organic search. The sky is essentially the limit when slicing and dicing customer value data.

The following portion of the terms of service for Google Analytics must be taken into account:

You won't (and won't permit any third party to) use the Service to track or collect personally identifiable information of Internet users. You will also not (and won't permit any third party to) associate any data gathered from Your website(s) (or such third parties website(s)) with any personally identifying details from any source as part of Your use (or such third parties use) of the Service.

I won't pretend to be a lawyer, but it is possible to interpret these terms as a violation of Google's terms of service. On the other side, one may argue that Google violates its terms of service by prominently displaying the Transaction ID in its interface, which is personally identifiable information.

If you are worried about Google's terms, you can always use a different web analytics tool. In addition, if you aggregate the data by customer segment rather than by individual customer, you are likely not in violation of the intent of this section. You must make the determination.

Customers often visit many sources before finalizing a purchase. Before completing a purchase, they may click on many paid efforts, an email campaign, and an organic link. 'Regardless of your strategy, you must consider that customers don't follow a straight path from one source to another on your website.

Which entity receives credit for the customer? You will need to determine which regulations apply. Many organizations I've dealt with consider the first source to "own" the customer. Still, they will reassign the account to another source if the consumer becomes inactive for an extended period (e.g., no purchases for six or more months).

If you use these methods to track customer lifetime value, you will discover that your decision-making is significantly improved. You can now measure the effectiveness of your marketing operations in great detail.

CHAPTER 9: UNIQUE SELLING PROPOSITIONS FOR YOUR BUSINESS IN DIFFICULT TIMES.

A recession doesn't need to cause trouble for your business. Even in thriving markets, there are ups and downs for every business.

Are you and your organization adequately prepared and equipped to tackle the demands of a soft or tough economy?

Many business owners fear the economic downturn and the risk of losing customers, employees, or profits. They believe that if the economy weakens, customers and customers would scale back on projects, cease spending and possibly even seek cheaper options from the competition.

This is true, but only to a limited extent. Certainly, a slowing economy and unfavorable consumer mood can challenge your organization or allow you to get new customers and increase your sales by adopting techniques that perform best in a declining market and are fantastic for times of market expansion.

Depending on your sector, you can employ different techniques to preserve and boost your sales while your competitors compete to survive.

The following USPs (Unique Selling Propositions) set quantifiable targets and identify critical strategic actions that will aid you in effectively navigating your firm through unpredictable economic times while others struggle to survive:

1. Utilize the quiet period to improve your company's fundamentals and fundamentals.

After a long operation, your firm requires tightening its knots and bolts and lubricating its moving parts to eliminate squeaks. Start at the top by reviewing and reaffirming your organization's values, vision and mission. Ensure that your employees are driven to uphold the company's values by showing a clear awareness of the business issues and expressing their contribution.

Align your company's objectives and values with the incentives and rewards for your employees. Distribute the information around the organization so that your employees can demonstrate initiative. Engage your staff in problem-solving and solicit their unique suggestions to increase profitability, improve efficiency and cut expenses.

2: Outthink the competitors.

Pause for a moment and ask yourself the following question: if what I sell or offer is substantially the same as that of my competitors, what do I need to be different and superior in different ways, including customer service, marketing, promotion, and sales?

Beyond creativity and innovation, the solution to this question lies in favorably differentiating your firm from its competition through "thinking leadership" and inspiring ingenuity, which must become second nature to you and your organization in hard times.

Your ultimate goal is to stand out fully in the minds of your customers by implementing innovative sales and marketing techniques to generate Unique Shining Points (USPs) that are exclusive to your company and the industry. In other words, your company must positively separate itself from its competitors or perish.

3: Reactivate Old Leads.

With minimal other sales effort, it is possible to convert old leads into productive companies. Many leads that you have abandoned in the past can be resurrected and converted if you persist.

In 2007, Harvard School of Business research indicated that most salespeople, regardless of industry, quit too soon. 75 percent of sales to businesses or customers are made on the fifth sales call, and 25 percent of salespeople make more than three sales calls!

4. Provide a superior level of service to your customers.

Holding on to your existing customers through difficult times is akin to holding fire in your hand; consequently, it is essential for the survival and longevity of your firm.

Maintaining a culture of sales-service excellence by going the other mile, satisfying customers, and offering them more value for their money is a surefire method to preserve the momentum of your organization. Now is the opportunity to go the other mile, which might be the difference between merely satisfying your customers and astounding them.

5. Plan and execute a bold new marketing plan.

To avoid a pause in your business from occurring in the first place, you must continuously and actively market throughout the entire year and every week. Not only when you need business. A continuing marketing plan assures a steady flow of new business leads. Marketing performed today initiates a sales cycle that will result in new business when you need it in six months.

6. Improve the value of your current products or services.

In a recession, buyers are more price-conscious than ever before. Therefore, address their worry by providing them with the most value for their money. There is no need to "give the store" or provide a degree of service that is excessive.

Your customers will see a small amount of other effort or service as a substantial value gain. Utilize technology and social media to stimulate business expansion while enhancing customer service, communication, and follow-up.

7: Be optimistic and enthused.

During slow business seasons, you must remain optimistic and avoid being despondent. People and consumers can sense your depression if you are depressed, which can negatively impact your internal and external business.

Don't lose hope; instead, be excited, have faith in your employees, your products, and your services, and transmit that spirit of passion and faith to your employees and consumers. Remember that you are not alone because, in a market downturn, everyone is under the same umbrella and experiencing the same circumstances as you.

Seek the assistance of a professional coach and mentor who can help you address your strengths and shortcomings, identify your inner motivation and realign your efforts with the broader picture.

8: Refrain from implementing any scheduled price hikes.

Even if you believe that a price rise is long overdue and that you deserve it, a business downturn isn't the ideal time to implement one. Adjust your prices during this temporary lull to suit a larger variety of customers.

9. Control negative and inept individuals in your organization.

Negative people can damage your achievement even in the greatest of circumstances. During difficult circumstances, the last thing you need is a negative or ineffective employee who does not share your values and corporate culture.

As it only takes one inept or negative employee to hold back an entire team, you must control and handle these situations with confidence and promptness and dismiss anyone who does not "buy into" your company's culture.

Summing up, there are defining periods in every business cycle and in every business person's career that call for extraordinary actions commensurate with the challenge at hand. However, businesspeople tend to lose sight of the big picture due to the stresses of difficult times.

Ensure that you and your team receive the appropriate coaching to focus on "back to basics" and push your team to the next level, where everyone is adept in the fundamentals and the basics.

Keep the larger picture in mind while developing the finest tactics, programs, and services to increase your revenues, position your firm for continued success, and, most importantly, truly separate your organization from its competitors in the market.

CHAPTER 10: HOW TO BOOST YOUR CUSTOMERS' PERCEPTION OF YOUR VALUE.

In the customer's mind, there is a mathematical equation that only they know: the equation of perceived advantages and perceived costs. The solution to this calculation is then compared to other "like" purchases or potential purchases to determine a value. Remember that this is all in the mind of the customer.

To observe this idea in action, recall your most recent significant purchase.

How did you decide to buy this specific product?

Did you conduct research?

Did the retailer or seller have only one brand or model, and you "settled" for it out of a sense of urgency?

Or are you an unyielding logician who won't compromise until you have the finest possible deal?

While merely scraping the surface, all these questions demonstrate that our purchasing decisions are influenced by many overlapping and intertwined functions within ourselves but ultimately hinge on our perception of value. If we see a bargain, we will purchase. Even if we desire or need the item, we won't purchase it if we believe it isn't a fair value and there is no sense of urgency.

Unfortunately, the value of your business isn't what you consider it to be but what your consumers perceive it to be.

If this is the case, what steps must you take to ensure that you add value to your customer's eyes? It might be as easy as giving other information or as complex as extending your business hours. Whatever the optimal answer may be, it will originate from customer feedback. Don't solely rely on demographic data and market research.

Even though these are essential pieces of the entire picture, relying solely on this information is the easy way out. Listen to your customers' complaints via surveys, follow-up calls, service interactions, and outreach functions to anticipate and address their requirements before they become a problem.

When you can boost your customers' sense of the value of your products and services, they will be more satisfied and more willing to tell others about their "excellent deal."

An inherent value should accompany everything you do for your customers. Unless your product is the best of its type in the world, you must compete with others who sell similar goods. Perhaps one of you will get a competitive advantage by providing the largest selection of these things.

A competitor may find a commercial advantage by offering in only select markets. Others may be able to undercut the competition by providing the lowest pricing feasible. However, one necessity and value is being neglected: each consumer's attention.

When customers exhibit interest in your product or service, they are, by extension, exhibiting interest in your company and you. There are moments in internet marketing when a million transactions can occur without a single human connection.

On the other hand, you can receive hundreds of thousands or millions of calls from confused customers on days when the technology itself is defective. By delivering exceptional service at this stage, you provide value to the product buyers are interested in, a quality that possibly no one else provides.

How often have you been compelled to pick between comparable products with equivalent prices?

What was the deciding factor?

The human element may be the deciding factor, even if it costs a few other dollars. Remember that most individuals are prepared to pay a little more to be handled uniquely.

Creating a demand among consumers is the crux of selling. You require that they require your products and services. You need them to want to return again and again. In today's incredibly competitive marketplaces, having an excellent product at a reasonable price is insufficient. The advantage will come from the traditional personal touch even in today's global, digital environment.

Once you have generated a compelling need for the items, you begin to add value to your consumers by treating them with a little extra care - what does it cost you to say Good Morning to a caller, even if you know the caller will complain?

It is completely free, but what does it provide in exchange? Perhaps a customer who called to complain about a minor issue leaves with their complaint resolved, merchandise in hand, and a discount while remaining loyal.

You have salvaged a sale and nearly guaranteed another sale with little more than a bit of time, a pleasant greeting, and a price reduction on a product. (Your marketing budget should be adaptable enough to accommodate these purchases regardless.) Essentially, you have spent nothing.

Especially when all marketing, sales, and other transactions are conducted online, the personal element in business is sometimes lacking. Even an email thanking a customer for a past transaction and inviting them to a future sales event is more than just a good idea; it is a must.

CHAPTER 11: PROMOTING ON "LOW PRICE" BUT "VALUE" IS ESSENTIAL FOR SUCCESS.

While a low price will typically increase sales volume, if you can't reduce unit cost simultaneously, you lose profit, and (the trumpets) the customers you attract through a low price will often defect when a competitor offers an even lower price. If you wish to keep your current customer, you can choose to promote "Added Value."

In actuality, value-added items or services often fetch a higher price that buyers are ready to pay than those with the lowest pricing. Use the following examples as inspiration to improve your business's value equation.

Add Value with "No Cost Extra Service": The vehicle was in the garage undergoing minor repairs. When picking up the vehicle, the customer was delighted to see that the carpets had been vacuumed for free.

Attached to the steering wheel was a business card that read, "We always vacuum the interior as part of our value-added service." By vacuuming the carpets, the garage brought a smile to the customer's face at almost no other cost.

Add Value with Velocity: Same-day clothing alterations, same-day shipment, five-minute loan applications, and glasses within one hour. Call when you are ready to depart, and your order will be waiting for you when you arrive.

Your furnace has just been repaired, and the provider provides value by calling to confirm that the job was completed correctly.

Improve Value through Communication: Send "Helpful Hints" regarding product use; design a newsletter; thank customers on product anniversaries (Wow! The age of your refrigerator is ten years! The florist reminds you of your mother's birthday, so why would you go elsewhere?

Add Value with Ambience: Fresh flowers in the welcome area; spotless restrooms; appropriate music; creative and appealing packaging, etc. A mint was presented gracefully after dinner (rather than tossed into a "grab bowl").

Added Value with Extra Information - They purchased a piece of equipment, and you email them once a month for years with tips, other applications, or innovative ways to enjoy their investment (it's okay to repeat tips but not too often).

There is no limit to the list of value-adding strategies. This week, I challenge you and your team to generate a list of ten possible strategies, select the most effective one and implement it.

The simple and laziest method of advertising is to reduce prices. It is far preferable to win people over with more value; they will gladly purchase from you if they perceive that they have received more for their money.

With This Method, You Can Create Immediate Customer Satisfaction And Significantly Increase Your Product's Value.

As an internet marketer, you have previously identified the market sector and market demand. You have a product or service for which you have established a price. You are prepared to sell it.

But wait..! You'd like to multiply the value of your product or service many times over but don't want your prospect to feel the pinch when purchasing it because even though the value of your product or service can be multiplied many times over, the payment for it remains the same!

What an anomaly!

Repeat the reading:

Even though you wish to multiply the value of your service or product by a significant amount, the price remains the same!

Notice the distinction?

Let me show you an example.

The idea is to "transform" your product or service's value into a "virtual product or service value."

Say I've written a popular ebook entitled "How to Find the Perfect Wife" and priced each copy at $98.00. This is the selling price. This is the ebook's selling price or current price at the moment of sale.

If instead of selling the ebook for $98.00, I develop a membership system in which the prospective buyer may join as a member and receive 200 credit points for $98.00, I have rapidly added value to the buyer's $98.00 investment.

With the 200 credit points (which he acquired for $98), he can purchase the popular ebook and will have 102 credit points remaining to buy additional products or services from you.

Observe what occurs immediately:

In exchange for $98, the prospect has received greater perceived value in credit points.

He receives his hot ebook and extra credit that he can use for other backend sales and pays the same $98.00.

By performing this straightforward action, you satisfy the customer and set the stage for future backend purchases.

Consider for a moment where else this notion can be applied.

Can it be integrated into your existing web marketing campaigns? This notion has limitless applications in offline and online marketing and the actual, non-virtual world.

However, when applied to your online marketing activities, it offers the flexibility to improve the value of your products and services without incurring any more costs. It increases revenue and produces instant customer delight. Does this concept currently have a place in your online marketing strategy?

CHAPTER 12: HOW A WEBSITE CAN INCREASE A COMPANY'S VALUE.

Due to the expense of designing a website, a small business may give its online presence little importance. There are, after all, many expenses that may appear to be of greater importance.

Priorities include inventory, equipment, stationery, and advertising, but without a website, the company is missing out on a rising percentage of customers who conduct product and service searches online.

There are many ways to recruit new customers, including printed telephone directories, leaflet distribution, newspaper and magazine advertisements, referrals from existing customers, business card distribution, internet searches, and online advertising.

A website can aid a small business in attracting new customers and increasing sales revenue. As the number of households having Internet access rises, the demand for printed business directories declines. People of all ages now conduct online searches while trying to purchase an item or hire a handyperson.

Before making a purchase, many computer users like to conduct internet research. A website can contain considerably more information than might be conveyed in a short print advertisement. A company's website could include product information, prices, technical specifications, stock availability, delivery choices, and customer reviews.

In addition to product and service information, other website elements might entice visitors to contact a business. A customer contact form enables anyone to input their email address, phone number, and inquiry data seven days a week and 24 hours a day. This is of enormous use to busy individuals who may be online late at night when telephone inquiries are unavailable. A location map will assist customers in locating business locations.

Signage for vehicles, business cards, printed stationery, and newspaper ads. Due to the extra value of having a website, the URL can be placed on all advertising materials. This encourages prospective customers to visit the website, place an online order or get sufficient information to inquire.

After deciding that a website is a good concept, a business could evaluate if it has the expertise, skills, and time to construct its web pages. If not, they should reach out to a web designer and pose the following questions:

• Does the desired domain name exist?

• What are your rates? There may be a fixed price per page, yearly domain registration fees, and monthly hosting and administrative fees.

• Will the web pages be optimized for search engines, and if so, is there another cost?

- What are the choices for updating web pages?

- What is the number of email addresses included?

- Will a map of the area be included?

- Will a form for customer inquiries be included?

- How many photos are permitted?

Considering what is required in a business website will aid in comparing the pricing of web designers and assist a firm in maximizing the benefits of its internet presence.

CHAPTER 13: STRATEGY AND CUSTOMER FOCUS.

Business success must begin and conclude with the consumer. Customer surplus is the difference between what a customer pays for a product and what they would pay for the product or the "worth" of the product.

In their efforts to grow their businesses, organizations have difficulty persuading customers to choose their products over those of their competitors, to purchase more of a product if they are already using it, and to give a new product a try.

Fundamentally, customers make purchases when they believe the price to be reasonable for the product's worth. Business strategy is largely concerned with creating value for the firm, which is impossible without creating customer value.

Strategy and an "appealing" value proposition must revolve around the customer's needs. A compelling value proposition may be more competitive than what they are now receiving from a rival and/or something entirely new where there is no competition.

The most effective plan isn't necessarily allowing us to defeat the opposition. It could also be the one that allows the company to avoid direct competition and provide higher consumer value.

A strategy to create superior value must be a two-step process, beginning with formulating a superior value proposition based on an in-depth understanding of consumer requirements. The second step is to build an effective and efficient value proposition delivery mechanism.

Putting the customer first, a winning strategy is formulated by asking questions about consumer wants and attempting to uncover the true motivations, goals, and requirements that customers seek to satisfy when purchasing products and services.

The best product/service offers are those in which the customer sees good value for the price paid, and the organization can achieve its desired profit margin.

Customer value creation comes first, followed by a competitive response. Wherever there is an opportunity to profit, competitors will appear. In addition to focusing on the consumer, a winning strategy must address the business's activities to counter potential competition responses and the market position it will adopt.

Often, the topic of strategy is presented as an integrative management system focusing on budgeting, vision statements, and performance indicators. However, if the firm does not maintain a focus on the customer and the market, all worksheets and PowerPoints won't lead to success.

"Value Added" - That Little Something Extra That Makes All The Difference.

What do you sell?

Are you the sole vendor of this product?

Why should I purchase it from you as opposed to someone else?

Seriously. why do people buy from you instead of someone else that offers the same product? If all other factors are equal, the answer is price, and when competing on price, no one wins.

If you lower your pricing to compete with a rival, he will likely do the same, and it will be your turn. It is a vicious circle in which no one wins, not even the consumer, because to cut your pricing to compete, you will likely have to reduce the quality of your service.

The solution to the issue is to develop a "value-added service" that differentiates you from the competition.

Do you provide a guarantee?

Do you deliver?

Will you sell reorders (in smaller quantities) at the same price as the initial order?

Do you offer complimentary shipping?

Are fries included with your meal?

Do you compensate loyal customers for their continued business?

Do you have a "frequent buyer's card?"

Find a way to distinguish yourself aside from the competitors, and you will be rewarded handsomely.

An associate in the flooring industry would take his largest customers annually on vacation. When he originally informed me about the plan, I asked him how he could afford to do something so extreme. He replied that his customers "are prepared to spend extra because they know they'll get a trip out of it."

What is your unique selling proposition?

I constantly consider transportation prices, shipping, and handling fees when I order online. Some firms, for whatever reason, demand another $5 to $10 as a "handling fee." They manage matters differently than their competition (who only charge for shipping).

Start by not trying to nickel-and-dime me to death if you want to "manage" my money (and the business of tens of thousands of other frugal consumers). If you want to differentiate yourself, offering free shipping is a simple beginning.

What about your returning customers?

Do you have any special plans for them?

Are you providing them with an "Oh, I'd miss it if I couldn't find someone else who." reason to stay with you? If not, locate one.

Do you send Christmas cards to your customers?

What about birthday cards?

Well, so does everyone else! Do you send Groundhog Day greeting cards to your customers? No? I can assure you that if you received a Groundhog's Day greeting card, you would remember it, and isn't that what you desire?

Find a way to offer value to your product or service; you won't only differentiate yourself from the competition but also give people a cause to buy from you!

CHAPTER 14: WAYS YOU CAN IMPROVE YOUR CUSTOMERS' EXPERIENCE.

Today, restaurant chains are similar in many ways, from the food they serve to the marketing techniques they employ to attract more consumers. Some emphasize their food, while others concentrate their marketing strategies on providing superior customer service.

Basic customer service is a factor that many food businesses overlook. They believe customers will continue to return and overlook their service if they deliver good cuisine.

Educated customers who know their fundamental rights and want the greatest value for their money don't overlook such simple considerations. Simply labeled "extra mile" services, these little gestures leave consumers satisfied and pleased.

The staff's attentiveness is another factor that encourages customers to return. While some diners take their time deciding on the menu, other patrons prefer receiving helpful recommendations, such as the restaurant's specialties, perennial favorites, and others. Some consumers like quiet attention, whereas others desire lively and friendly attention.

Although it is standard for a restaurant to have someone greet customers at the front door, opening the doors for them and leading them to an empty table will impress them. However, giving them a perfect spot in the dining area, such as a breathtaking view of the sunset, will make them feel even more special.

While waiting for the main meal, offering complimentary appetizers shows that restaurant owners are interested in maximizing earnings and establishing a pleasant, mutually beneficial connection with their customers. A modest dish of garlic stick bread or almonds and the like does not harm the businessman's wallet, and the smiles painted on the children's faces are unparalleled and priceless.

Restaurant managers or owners occasionally engage with regulars and address them by name, fostering a warmer, more personal relationship that isn't just focused on a profitable customer-business relationship.

Attention to their demands is the essential factor, as customers have a wide array of wants that someone with a great eye for minute details can only perceive.

Customers have different moods and attitudes, preferences, and quirks. Still, a basic understanding of customer service and the different types of customers will guide restaurant owners, managers, and the entire team in dealing with them most effectively at the most appropriate time.

Choose only the finest restaurant supplies, as dining should always be a feast for the tongue and the eyes. World-class restaurant supplies and equipment are accessible online, seven days a week and 24 hours a day, so you don't have to drive far to satisfy your restaurant's needs.

How can you increase your value?

1. Be Specific Regarding Your Offering.

Before contributing other values, you must be aware of your value and natural talents and gifts. Respond to these questions. "What do my ideal customers hope to benefit from working with me?" "How are my personality, purpose, and abilities distinctive?"

How can I effectively leverage my strengths to deliver the benefits desired by my target customers?

2. Be Bright Where You Are.

Utilize your special skills to convey the rewards customers desire. If you are inspiring, then be inspiring. If you are specific, be specific and give them what they desire. Customers purchase you as part of a package, so be confidently authentic. They'll adore it.

3. See The Future.

Ask prospects about their desires. Participate in their vision. Once you've determined this is a suitable fit, explain why you are an ideal candidate. Paint a picture for them of what you observe. Get thrilled about the possibility of collaboration and co-creating their dream! If they bore you, refer them to another person.

4. Donate Greater Than You Receive.

Add other value for the pure pleasure of giving! Always surpass the agreed-upon value. Provide information, tools, resources, and recommendations. Become a resource for your customers and potential customers. They will sing your praises.

5. Be Happy.

Always and only, ENJOY YOURSELF! Joy is contagious, and customers like the company of happy, enthusiastic individuals. Remember that the more value you contribute to the world, the more you will get in return.

When everyone donates from the heart, the world will be transformed!

Create riches for others by simply (and effectively) being yourself.

CHAPTER 15: TIPS FOR ADDING EXTRA VALUE FOR YOUR CUSTOMERS.

You can provide other value if you create a business and want to attract more customers. Instead of focusing on what you desire from current and potential customers, emphasize the value you can deliver to them.

When women visit the cosmetics counter at a department store or have a facial, they adore receiving small sample presents of items. The same holds for your customers. They enjoy receiving small "samples" or extras. It helps them feel special and cherished.

What simple, enjoyable, and easy-to-create items might you give your customers that would have a significant impact? The possibilities are unlimited if you use your imagination! Examples include a newsletter, an article or list of tips, a checklist or quiz, a small amount of other time, a referral, an invitation to your seminar, a bookmark, or a handcrafted journal.

Newsletters, articles, and Tips.

I believe newsletters are the most effective method for establishing relationships with prospective customers. Over time, individuals come to know, like, and trust you and are willing to conduct business with you.

According to marketing experts, people must see or hear your name or services at least seven times before they are willing to purchase from you. A newsletter is a great way to maintain contact and provide value simultaneously.

Email newsletters are now widespread, and with today's technology, they are both simple and inexpensive. You need not write a lengthy article; you can begin with a simple list of suggestions.

Checklists and Quizzes.

Creating customized checklists and quizzes for my customers has been enjoyable. People enjoy taking 20-question quizzes with 'yes/no' or 'on a scale of one to ten answers. These are simple to create for your customers, who will find great value in them.

Ask yourself, "What are the top ten things my customers want, and what are the top ten problems they're facing?" Create a list combining the needs and obstacles and have a simple, ready-made customized evaluation.

Depending on your customer, the title could be "Are you very healthy as you could be?" or "Is your life in harmony?" Or, "Do you possess the qualities of a successful entrepreneur?" You have the concept.

Extra Time.

Offer a customer experiencing exceptional difficulty another 10 to 15 minutes of your time. Inform them that you are granting them another time so they won't expect it every time, or check in with them by phone or email between sessions to determine their progress.

They will greatly appreciate your interest, and it won't require much of your time. In addition, it's great to offer them a little extra time, an email, or a handwritten note to celebrate their success.

Recommendation to Your Network.

Your marketing strategy for growing your business should include expanding your network and database. You can leverage your network by acting as a resource for your customers and referring them to individuals who provide their required services. Your customer may mention that they need a good accountant or that they experienced back pain after playing tennis and are looking for a good chiropractor.

Here is your opportunity to recommend the professionals you know. Your customer will greatly value the fact that you have an extensive network of personal contacts. It is advisable to provide multiple names so they can choose who to work with independently.

A Request to Attend Your Seminar.

Invite customers to your seminars and workshops for free or at a discounted price. Inform customers they will be the first to learn about your upcoming talks and seminars. People will feel like they are in your "inner circle" if they are the first to know.

Offer them an incentive or referral fee for bringing a friend or colleague, such as a 20% discount for each person they refer who registers. If they bring five guests, they receive free admission. It provides them with an incentive and assists them in filling your workshop. It could be the best money you will ever spend on advertising your business, and it's free.

You'll feel better when consistently providing other value to your customers, and your business will grow rapidly!

CONCLUSION.

Creating exceptional customer value is essential in determining a company's success. No matter how much you charge, your consumers want to feel they are receiving the best value for their time and money. Even more so, they want to believe that the freebies you provide them are of exceptional value.

By improving the value of your products and services, you can simultaneously increase the prices you charge for them and your earnings. Here are some suggestions for establishing and enhancing the customer value of your products and services:

Always Exceed Your Customers' Expectations: By exceeding your customers' normal expectations, you will significantly improve the value they perceive you to have provided. The more valuable your customers view you and your firm to be, the greater the quality of the information or work you supply them.

Don't Be Like Everyone Else: Be unique. Many markets are oversaturated with identical products and services with little to no differentiation from the competition.

There are many ways to differentiate yourself from your competitors. You can package your goods differently than competitors. You can devise a sales strategy that isn't the same as everyone else's.

There are many ways to distinguish yourself from the herd. You can design information products to appear differently than those of your competitors. You can ensure that your sales system is straightforward and user-friendly.

A disproportionate number of businesses in every field don't care about customer service. As long as you purchased their product, they have no interest in whether or not you had a positive experience with their firm.

Customers like to do business with companies that give superior customer service. The good news is that you can benefit from this. It affords you the ability to supply the lacking excellent customer service. You can significantly raise the perceived worth of your products and services in the minds of your customers. Always, always provide excellent customer service!

Establishing relationships is the essence of business. Your customers and customers value long-term relationships. Your company becomes more than just a place to purchase goods by doing so. You become a valued friend and advisor to whom they may approach with queries and problems. If you consistently provide this, you will have loyal customers for life.

Add Extra Value: This one appears evident based on the article's title. If you and your competitor offer the same product at the same price, you must ask yourself why a customer would decide to purchase from you rather than your competitor.

Unless you add more value to the transaction, such as superior after-sales service or longer return terms than your competitors, the customer won't view your company differently from the others.

Providing exceptional customer value will distinguish your company from the competition! Nowadays, competition is harsh and brutal, and you must offer yourself every possible advantage to win in your industry.

Management Skills for Managers.

1. Time Management for Managers
2. Employee Coaching for Managers
3. Team Building for Managers
4. Self Confidence for Managers
5. Negotiation Skills for Managers
6. Customer Service Skills for Managers
7. Assertiveness for Managers
8. Business Etiquette for Managers
9. Listening Skills for Managers
10. Leadership Skills for Managers
11. Communication Skills for Managers
12. Presentation Skills for Managers
13. Stress Management for Managers
14. Decision Making for Managers
15. Conflict Management for Managers.

Series: Financial Freedom at Any Age.

- Achieving Financial Freedom in your 20's
- Achieving Financial Freedom in your 30's
- Achieving Financial Freedom in your 40's
- Achieving Financial Freedom in your 50's
- Achieving Financial Freedom in your 60's
- Achieving Financial Freedom in your 70's and beyond.
- Achieving Financial Freedom in children
- Achieving Financial Freedom in teenagers
- Achieving Financial Freedom in college students.
- Financial Scams to be Aware of in Retirement.

Series: Personal Finance for You.
- ➢ Buying and Selling Crypto for Beginners
- ➢ Why Investing in Dividend Stocks Makes Sense.

Series: Wealth 2022.

- ➢ Online Entrepreneurship.
- ➢ Starting Your Own Business
- ➢ Wealth Management
- ➢ Passive Income.
- ➢ 12 Steps to Starting your own business.

Series: Excellent Customer Service.

- ➢ Excellent Customer Service in Retail
- ➢ Excellent Customer Service in Fast Food
- ➢ Excellent Customer Service in Full-Service Restaurant
- ➢ Excellent Customer Service in Teaching.
- ➢ Excellent Customer Service in Real Estate
- ➢ Excellent Customer Service in a Call Center
- ➢ Excellent Customer Service as a Receptionist
- ➢ Excellent Customer Service in a Hotel
- ➢ Excellent Customer Service in Selling
- ➢ Excellent Customer Service No Matter the Situation.

- ➢ Excellent Customer Service in Dental Office
- ➢ Excellent Customer Service in Medical Office.

Series: Quick Money.

- ➢ Quick Money in a Week
- ➢ Quick Money in a Weekend
- ➢ Quick Money in a Month
- ➢ Quick Money for Students.

Series: How to Promote.

- ➢ How to Promote your Recipe Book
- ➢ How to Promote your Children's Book.

Other books by D.K. Hawkins.

- ➢ How to Make Your Business Thrive During a Recession
- ➢ Creating Surplus Value for Customers
- ➢ Recognizing Opportunities to Increase Cash Flow.

Author Bio

D.K. Hawkins. D.K. enjoys reading personal business books as well as spending time outdoors. More books will come in this collection, so please follow on Amazon for more books.

Thank you for your purchase of this book.

I honestly do appreciate it and appreciate you, my excellent customer.

God Bless You.

D.K. Hawkins.

www.ingramcontent.com/pod-product-compliance
Lightning Source LLC
Chambersburg PA
CBHW050009230526
45465CB00003BB/1336